To Andrey
with lots of love
Jemima

Dec '93

D1356247

BOOK OF
Lavender

BOOK OF
Lavender

JACKIE FRENCH

HarperCollins*Publishers*

First published in 1993
by HarperCollins Publishers
London

First published in Australia in 1993 by
Angus&Robertson, an imprint of HarperCollins Publishers

© *Jackie French 1993*

A CIP catalogue record for this book is available
from the British Library

ISBN 0 00 412895-8
Printed in Hong Kong

CONTENTS

LAVENDER

A HARDY HERB

And still she slept an azure-lidded sleep,
In blanched linen, smooth and lavender

~

KEATS, *THE EVE OF SAINT AGNES*

Lavender has no equal. It is endlessly generous, fragrant and hardy. Its soft grey cloud of leaves lends a gentleness to a garden— often a relief from the strident greens and reds and yellows. The scent of lavender evokes sunshine, and hot soil, and bees in warm gardens.

Perhaps the hardiest herb, lavender loves limy, dry, exposed soils; it will also thrive in rich, moist, acid gardens, though it won't tolerate wet feet or too much shade. Exposed hillsides, salt-laden winds, heat, drought and moderate frost— lavender accepts all of them happily and gives back endless fragrance.

Lavender is a flavouring as well as a perfume. It can be delicious and used to be much more popular than it is today. Like many flower flavours lavender has simply gone out of fashion, but it is still much nicer than elderly cinnamon or cloves, or artificial vanilla for custards and icings.

Lavender has been valued over the centuries (it was said to have been brought out of the Garden of Eden by Adam and Eve), not just for its beauty and fragrance, but also as a culinary herb and for its medicinal properties. Its botanical name, *Lavandula,* comes from the Latin *lavare,* to wash, and lavender was used as an antiseptic wash for wounds, as a fragrant wash for pleasure, and as an insecticide wash to repel lice, fleas, mosquitoes, bedbugs and other household pests. Roman beds had special posy holders that held lavender to deter bedbugs. Virgil mentions lavender in both the Bucolics and the Georgics.

Lavender's use as a flavouring has only recently gone out of fashion— perhaps because its gentle sweetness can't compete with our aggressively sweetened and flavoured foods.

Lavender and Orange Salad

SERVES 2

~ 3 *very ripe oranges, sliced, with the pith and membrane removed*

~ 1 *tspn chopped fresh lavender flowers*

~ 3 *tspns red wine vinegar*

~ *a very little chopped Spanish onion*

Mix all the ingredients together. Serve as a first course.

Lavender oil (mainly found in the calyx or seed case) is mildly sedative, antiseptic and analgesic. It has been prescribed for everything from the bites of mad dogs, to baldness and snakebite— none of which are helped much by lavender— and more successfully, for carsickness, insomnia, fevers and migraine.

The scent of lavender is said to be relaxing and stimulating at the same time. It aids concentration by relieving stress. Queen Elizabeth I is said to have consumed up to 10 cups of lavender water a day to relieve migraine.

Lavender Stuffing for Roast Lamb

~ 1 *cup (2 oz) soft breadcrumbs*

~ 1 *egg*

~ 1 *onion, chopped*

~ 1 *tspn very finely chopped lavender flowers*

~ 1 *tspn chopped rosemary flowers*

Mix all the ingredients together.

*'Here's flowers for you,
Hot lavender, mints, savoury, marjoram. . .'*

~

WILLIAM SHAKESPEARE, THE WINTER'S TALE

Lavender Kebabs

❧

This is a Moroccan recipe.

Pound well-dried lavender in a mortar with a little salt and lemon juice, then marinate chunks of lamb in the resulting powder. Grill (broil) over an open fire. Toss lavender branches onto the fire to increase the scent and taste.

Lavender Baked Custard

❧

SERVES 2–4

~ *1 bunch lavender*

~ *2 cups (16 fl oz) cream*

~ *½ cup (4 oz) caster sugar*

~ *3 eggs, beaten*

Gently heat the lavender in the cream for 10 minutes. Cool and strain. Add the caster sugar and eggs and bake in a moderate oven (190°C/375°F) until set.

This custard is pale green but it tastes delicious.

Most cottage gardens had lavender bushes— they were hardy, and grew easily from neighbours' cuttings— and were invaluable for all aspects of domestic economy. In addition to repelling, lavender was used to flavour custards; it helped soothe a teething child and grandma's aching rheumatism. Women could also feed their men lavender-flavoured 'kissing comfits' to arouse their interest after a hard day in the fields.

Lavender was said to be a charm against the devil and was used in much the same way as garlic was used to deter vampires. Lavender flowers were hung on doors in the shape of a cross, and Irish brides wore a garter of lavender to protect them against witchcraft. A suitor with dishonourable intentions was repelled if a woman carried a nosegay of lavender.

To find your true love, try brewing lavender flowers and thyme in honey and wine. Drink the brew at bedtime — and dream well.

Lavender was also supposed to ensure chastity. A sprig of lavender was placed in the shoes of a wandering lover, or they were fed lavender-scented cakes. Lavender in the mattress ensured fidelity, as well as freedom from fleas and bedbugs, which might also have helped to make the marriage happier.

Lavender and
Champagne Sorbet
SERVES 4

~ 1 cup (8 fl oz) white wine
~ 1 cup (8 fl oz) water
~ juice of 2 lemons
~ 4 egg whites well beaten
~ 1 cup (7 oz) caster
(superfine) sugar
~ ½ cup stalkless lavender
flowers, dried in the oven or
microwave and crumbled to
powder

Blend all the ingredients till
well mixed. Freeze the
mixture, stirring every 20
minutes during the freezing
process. Serve slightly slushy.

Bavarian farmers tied bunches of lavender to their
cows' horns to ensure that the elves blessed them
with sweet milk.

A bowl of lavender was traditionally brought
indoors every winter's evening and left by the fire
for the scent to evaporate and fill the room. A few
lavender twigs were thrown on the fire before
bedtime to remove the stale smell of soot the next
day. Lavender oil was also thrown into the fire by
canny cooks to mask the smell of a burnt dish.
Lavender has symbolised both love and distrust.

King Charles II and his mistress Nell Gwyn
exchanged sachets of lavender, as did other lovers
of their time; but the asp that killed Cleopatra is
said to have been found under a lavender bush.
Wild lavender can still be found growing around
the Mediterranean region, and from the Canary
Islands to India, Pakistan and Somalia. On hot
days its fragrance fills the air— just as it can in
your garden.

A Potpourri for Relaxation

A combination of these perfumes is said to have a relaxing effect.

~ 6 cups lavender flowers

~ 2 cups dried lemon verbena leaves

~ 1 cup dried hop flowers

~ ½ cup dried camomile flowers

~ ¼ cup orris root

A Potpourri for Concentration

Keep a bowl of this potpourri on your desk, or give a jar to a friend.

~ 6 cups lavender flowers

~ 1 cup dried rosemary leaves

~ ¼ cup thyme leaves

~ 1 cup dried mint leaves

~ 3 tspns grated nutmeg

~ ¼ cup orris root

A Sweet Water

Take a gallon of spring water, 3 handfulls of roses, a handfull of lavender flowers, as much sweet marjoram, the pelling of six oranges, 12 cloves, bruise all these and put to them one ounce of orrice powder, 4 ounce of benjamin. Put all these into a rose still and draw off the first quart by itself and then a pint, you may draw after that another water from the lees which serve for present use but not for keep, and in the quart bottle 12 pennyworth of musk, and in the pint bottle 6 pennyworth tied up in bags and a little juniper sliced very thin as much as will lay on half a crown, 2 or 3 spoonfulls will sweeten a bason of water: keep it stop't very close; it will keep a year or 2.

The Book of Simples, circa 1650

To Make a Special Sweet Water to Perfume Clothes in the Folding Being Washed

Take a quart of damask rose water and put it into a glasse, put into it a handfull of Lavender flowers, two ounces of Orris, a dram of Muske, the weight of four pence of amber-greece, as much civet, four droppes of oyle of cloves, stop this close, and set it in the sunne a fortnight; put one spooneful of this water into a bason of common water and put it into a glasse and so sprinkle your clothes therewith in your folding.

Delights for Ladies, Sir Hugh Platt, 1594

To Make Sweet Water

Take damask roses at discretion, Basil, sweet marjoram, lavender, Wallnut leafs, of each two handfulls, Rosemary one handful, a little balm, Cloves, cinnamon, Bay leafs, Limon and Orange pills of each a few; pour apon these as much white wine as will conveniently wet them and let them infuse ten or twelve days; then distill it off.

Choice and Experimented Receipts, Sir Kenelm Digby, 1668

Lavender was one of the earliest perfumes. The Roman perfume 'nardinum' was made of pounded lilies, lavender and myrrh, and one of the perfume jars in Tutankhamun's tomb contained lavender.

The early name for lavender was 'Indian spike' — the Queen of Sheba offered Solomon 'myrrh, frankincense, spike. . .', and the biblical heroine Judith anointed herself with lavender before seducing and murdering the Assyrian commander Holofernes.

Lavender water is said to have been invented by the Benedictine Abbess Hildegarde at Bingen on the Rhine in the twelfth century. Lavender water gained its 'spinsters and white linen' reputation in Victorian times. Queen Victoria had all the rooms of her residences perfumed with lavender, and the wooden surfaces were polished with lavender oil.

Before that the scent of lavender was thought to be sexy.

Charlemagne demanded that lavender be planted in the royal gardens to ensure that he had a continual supply of lavender water. Louis XIV had his shirts rinsed in lavender, nutmeg and marjoram water. Madame de Pompadour washed in a bath of milk, honey, lavender and rose petals.

Eau de Cologne, with its citrus and lavender scent, was one of Napoleon's favourite perfumes. He renamed it Eau de Imperial and used it lavishly.

The most commonly grown lavender for commercial perfume production is *Lavandula* x *intermedia*, or *lavadin*, a cross between *Lavandula angustifolia* (English lavender) and *Lavandula latifolia* (Dutch lavender, or spike). The parent species are also widely used for perfumery. Dutch lavender produces an inferior oil, called 'spike lavender oil'.

Lavender oil is extracted by steam distillation. The best oil, and the one that has the least of camphor, is found in plants grown above 1000 metres (3000 feet), in the southern French Alps and northern Tasmania.

An Easy Way to Distill Lavender

This will not produce pure lavender oil but the perfume will still be wonderful.

Fill an old kettle with lavender flowers and leaves. (Make sure it is an old kettle as the scent may linger.) Place a piece of hose on the spout, fill the kettle with water and bring to the boil. Reduce to a simmer and catch the steam from the hose in a jar. The oil will evaporate first, leaving a wonderfully fragrant oil and water mix.

To Scent a Room with Lavender

~ Place a bowl of lavender by the window for the sun to draw out the scent.

~ Drop a little lavender oil on the light bulb of a table lamp— it will evaporate and fill the room with perfume.

~ Keep a pot of lavender and water simmering on the stove.

~ Throw bunches of lavender onto an open fire.

~ Place bowls of lavender-scented potpourri near doorways to help repel mosquitoes.

~ Place lavender oil in a porous jug so the perfume seeps into the room.

~ Place sprigs of lavender with other flowers in vases.

Potpourri

Lavender is one of the classic ingredients of potpourri. Its scent can perfume a room, remove mustiness, improve concentration and help you to relax. It can also repel mosquitoes and fleas— or just be a sudden delight when you lift the lid on a jar of potpourri.

Potpourri can either be made in a deep bowl or, even better, placed in a jar with a lid and left to mature for several months. Matured potpourri has a richer aroma, though you may find it difficult to wait that long before you smell it.

Insect-Repellent Potpourri

6 cups dried lavender flowers
1 cup dried rose petals
½ cup dried cloves
1 cup dried mint leaves
½ cup dried wormwood leaves
½ cup dried feverfew flowers
the dried peel of an orange and a lemon
½ cup orris root

Mix all the ingredients together. Place bowls of insect-repellent potpourri near doors and windows, or by your chair. Sew it into sachets to keep in drawers or cupboards.

The Celestial Bed

This was the invention of 'Dr' Graham, a prominent eighteenth-century charlatan. He advertised a bed that was perfumed 'with Arabian spices in the style of those of the seraglio of the Grand Turk'. The mattress contained neither feathers nor flock, but lemon balm, rose petals, lavender flowers and 'the hair from the tails of full-blooded black stallions to ensure virility'.

Which Lavender?

Lavender and Almond Sweets

There are about 30 species of lavender, and many more cultivated varieties, including the green lavender of the above song.

English Lavender

Old English Lavender (Lavandula angustifolia, *also known as* L. vera *or* L. officinalis)

This is the traditional small grey-leaved bush, with rich lavender-blue flowers and an even richer perfume. It grows to about 90 cm (35½ in), and has square stems. It will tolerate cold and temperate climates but doesn't do well in the subtropics or tropics, or in very humid climates. Old English lavender flowers in summer and the flowers will last for months. Bees love them; so do children. An old cottage tradition is to dry handkerchiefs on a hedge of English lavender.

16
~

White Lavender (Lavandula angustifolia *var.* alba)

A small, rather temperamental lavender, growing to about 60 cm (24 in). It has grey-white leaves and pure white flowers and a sweet fragrance. It will not tolerate extremes of cold, dryness, periods of extended rain, or very heavy frosts. It also seems to grow more slowly than other lavenders.

Pink Lavender (Lavandula angustifolia *var.* nana rosea*)*

A dwarf lavender with silver-grey leaves and greyish pink flowers. Pink lavender sounds pretty— and it is— but it isn't as spectacular as you might think. The flowers blend with the foliage and are often hard to distinguish.

Lavender and Almond Sweets

Mix 1 part dried crumbled lavender flowers with 4 parts marzipan. Shape into small balls then roll in almond meal with a little orange zest added. Leave to dry before storing.

These are very good.

Lavender Syllabub

SERVES 4

~ *2 tbspns dried lavender flowers, crumbed*

~ *3 cups (24 fl oz) cream*

~ *⅓ cup (3 oz) caster (superfine) sugar*

~ *juice of 1 lemon*

~ *a dash of brandy*

Whip all the ingredients together until thick. Pour into glasses and serve chilled.

The syllabub will be a lovely mauve-green colour.

Munstead (left) and Hidcote Purple (right) Lavenders

Bosdisto's Lavender

This variety has very large flower spikes of a deep rich blue.

Hidcote Purple

A semi-dwarf lavender, reaching to about 60 cm (24 in). It has silver-grey leaves and violet-blue flowers which hold their colour well when dried. Hidcote Purple is perhaps the best lavender for flower arrangements. It is also a good edging lavender and it has a wonderful scent to preserve in posies and sachets.

Miss Donnington

This is a very old form of English lavender, with pretty, deep-blue flowers.

Monastery Blue

A low-growing edging lavender with deep mauve flower spikes.

Mottisfont Abbey

A late flowering lavender, very fragrant, with pale lavender flower spikes. It was grown from a seed at Mottisfont Abbey in England.

Munstead or Dwarf Lavender

This was named for the famous gardener Gertrude Jekyll, who had a cottage garden at Munstead. Gertrude Jekyll loved to edge paths with Munstead lavender, and Munstead had been famous for centuries for its lavender.

Munstead lavender is low-growing, very compact and pretty, with grey-green leaves and intensely blue flowers— perhaps the deepest blue of all lavender flowers. Munstead lavender also flowers earlier than most lavenders. It is one of the best species for edging paths or gardens.

FRENCH LAVENDER

French Lavender (Lavandula dentata *var.* candicans*)*

This is an incredibly vigorous lavender. It grows to 90 cm (35½ in) and has finely toothed grey foliage. It flowers several times during the year, in both winter and summer. The flowers are long lasting, so one bush may appear to flower all through the year. The blooms are bluish lavender, on long stems.

Both the leaves and flowers of French lavender are fragrant, unlike English lavender, where the flowers are much more fragrant than the leaves.

French lavender will tolerate moderate frosts (ours tolerate temperatures down to -5°C (15°F)), though in very cold areas it can be grown as a pot plant and taken indoors.

Green French Lavender (Lavandula dentata *sp.)*

A smaller, less vigorous French lavender, with smaller, greener, softer leaves.

French Lavender

Italian Lavender, Spanish Lavender (Lavandula stoechas*)*
An upright plant with very thin-leaved foliage, silver grey and very
fragrant. Like French lavender, Italian lavender leaves are gloriously
scented, either fresh or dried. The flowers are deep purple throughout
winter and spring. Italian lavender was probably the lavender best
known to the ancient Greeks, Romans and Arabs and was used as an
antiseptic as well as an insecticide, and for perfumery. It needs
protection from harsh frost.
Italian lavender grows easily from seeds. Because of this it has become a
weed in some areas, so be careful where you plant it.

Pendunculata Lavender (Lavandula stoechas *var.* pendunculata*)*
This is one of my favourite lavenders. It has pale blue flowers and green,
delicate leaves that seem to droop. In contrast, other lavenders look
harsh and spiky. It is fast growing but won't tolerate heavy frost and
seems to take less readily from cuttings than other lavenders.

Italian (left) and Pendunculata (right) Lavenders

Green Lavender (Lavandula viridis, Lavandula stoechas *var.* viridis*)*

This should not be confused with Green French Lavender. The leaves are green, as are the bracts, but the flowers themselves are a dull white. The stems are grooved and covered with small hairs. Both leaves and flowers are fragrant, with a hint of spice and rosemary as well as classic lavender.

Green Lavender can be temperamental and is slow growing. It is perhaps a lavender only for the enthusiast— or one who wants to have the 'green lavender' of the nursery rhyme.

Green Lavender is native to the Pyrenees.

Green (left) and Mitcham (right) Lavenders

Mitcham Lavender (Lavandula *x* allardii)

An incredibly vigorous lavender, often sprawling and very fast growing. It takes almost invariably from cuttings and makes a quick and lovely hedge. The leaves are also fragrant and the flowers are long, pale blue spikes.

❧

Canary Island Lavender (Lavandula canariensis*)*

A frost-tender lavender with ferny leaves and bright blue winter flowers.

Lavender Cheeses

❧

SERVES 2–6

~ 1½ dried lavender flowers, crumbled

~ 500 g (8 oz) ricotta

~ 2 tbspns caster (superfine) sugar

~ ½ cup (4 fl oz) cream

~ grated zest of 1 orange and 1 lemon

Mix all the ingredients together. Pour the mixture into a clean cloth and leave to hang in a cool place for 48 hours. Unwrap and serve with more cream.

The lavender cheese will be round and fragrant, and quite delicious.

Fern-leafed Lavender

Woolly Lavender (Lavandula lanata)

A small, hairy lavender, growing to about 90 cm (35½ in). The flowers are deep purple.

Fern-leafed Lavender (Lavandula multifida)

Fern-leafed lavender has divided, fern-like leaves and tall spikes of bright, blue-violet winter flowers. It will tolerate mild but not heavy frost.

DUTCH LAVENDER

Spikenard, Spica, Spike (Lavandula latifolia, or L. spica)

This species has silver grey, largish leaves and fat, dark purple flowers. The scent is not quite as clear as English lavender, with a hint of camphor and spice as well. It is, however, incredibly fragrant, and one of the main perfume lavenders.

Lavandula citriodora

A rare lavender, with lemon-scented leaves.

Lavandula burmanii

Foliage of this species is similar to that of English lavender, with lavender coloured flowers and a spicy, camphor-like fragrance.

GROWING LAVENDER

*These herbes do grow wilde in Spaine, in Languedoc in France,
and the Island called the Stoechades aver against Massiliu; we
have them in our gardens and kept with great diligence from the
unjurie of our cold climate. . .*

~

GERARD, *HERBAL*, 1597.

Lavender is a very tolerant plant. It prefers limy,
well-drained soil but will grow in almost any
garden. It won't tolerate shade or semi-shade and
can be prone to powdery mildew in humid or
shady spots. There's not much you can do about
diseased lavender except take healthy cuttings
and plant them somewhere else.

Lavender grows quickly from seeds, though they
can be slow to germinate. They grow reasonably
true to type — you may be lucky and produce a
new lavender.

Lavender Ice-cream

SERVES 2–4

~ 2 cups lavender flowers

~ 2 cups (16 fl oz) cream

~ 6 egg yolks

~ ½ cup (4 oz) caster
(superfine) sugar

Heat the lavender flowers and
cream for 20 minutes without
letting it come to the boil.
Strain the mixture and add
the egg yolks and sugar. Heat
gently until the mixture coats
the back of a spoon; don't
allow it to simmer or boil.
Freeze till just set. Mix once
or twice while freezing if you
do not have an ice-cream
churn.

Lavender ice-cream is good
served with thin chocolate
biscuits, or chocolate leaves.

Cuttings of lavender grow even faster than seeds. Take cuttings from snappable wood, preferably from a low branch, and thrust it in sandy or well-drained soil in autumn or spring. Transplant in about 6 months' time.

Soft tip cuttings can be taken in spring, but they may not take; hardwood cuttings are much more reliable.

Another way to propagate lavender is by layering. Mound soil over a low branch and cut it off the main stem about 6 months later.

Prune lavender bushes every year— or at least every few years— to stop them from becoming untidy and too woody. Woody stems can break down and the plant will die. Use the prunings in potpourri, to make perfumes, to cook with— or throw them in the fire for a wonderful fragrance. Don't try and compost them because their high oil content will slow the compost down. They are, however, an excellent mulch around established plants to stop weed seeds germinating.

Young lavender plants need to be watered. Older bushes need very little, if any, watering or feeding. Slower growing bushes seem to live longer.

WHERE TO GROW LAVENDER

as a low border around gardens or along paths

as a thick hedge to keep out dogs and cats

in old-fashioned knot gardens or physic gardens or herb wheels

in pots on a windowsill

in giant tubs by the front door, where passers-by will brush against them

as a hedge by the clothesline— place handkerchiefs and underwear on
the hedge to dry

'Conserve of the Flowers of Lavender'
*Take the flowers being new so many as you please, and beat them with three times their weight
of white sugar, after the same manner as rosemary flowers; they will keep one year.'*

~

THE QUEEN'S CLOSET OPENED BY W. M., COOK TO QUEEN HENRIETTA MARIA 1655.

Lavender Punch

SERVES 2–6

~ juice of 3 lemons

~ 6 cups (1½ l) pineapple juice

~ 1 tspn chopped lavender

~ 1 bottle (750 ml) ginger ale

~ sugar to taste (you may not need any)

Combine all the ingredients and serve very cold, with ice.

Lavender Liqueur

~ 1 part camomile flowers

~ 3 parts lemon balm

~ 3 parts lemon grass

~ 1 part lavender flowers

~ 1 part rose hips

~ 1 part hop flowers (optional)

~ 1 part sugar

Mix all the ingredients. Cover with brandy and leave in a cool dark place (not the refrigerator) for 3 months. Strain and rebottle.

This is very relaxing before bedtime.

MEDICINAL LAVENDER

and the sicke man alos broughte into daunger

~

GERARD, *HERBAL*, 1597

An Excellent Water for the Head and For Sleep Called Ye Emperour Charles Water

When roses are blown, take a good quart of aquavitae in a glass with a narrow neck and when the roses are half blown take a handful of the leaves without ye seed, put them into the glass and when the marjoram bloweth and the Apiasstrum, take then a handful of their buds, chop them small and put them into the glass. Take also Cloves, Nutmegs, Cinnamons, mace, cardomum, of these an ounce and a half: bruise all these grossly and put in the glass and when the lavender and rosemary are blown add a handful of these flowers also; shake them well together and stop it close; let it stand ten days in a hot sun; it must be used by annointing the temples and nostrells; it fortifieth and corroboratest the head and memory.

The Book of Simples, circa 1650

A Lavender Liqueur

Lavender is a mild sedative and cough suppressant. It also has antiseptic properties, and can lower blood pressure. It is used externally as a stimulant added to massage oil to counteract arthritic or rheumatic pain or sprains or aches.

Too much lavender oil, however, is toxic. *Never use more than 2 drops at a time internally, and keep bottles of lavender oil out of the reach of children.* It is best to dilute pure lavender oil straightaway with other oil, or in whatever recipe you plan to use it.

LAVENDER OIL FOR CUTS

Shake a few drops of lavender oil in a little water and sponge it on the cut or graze.

Lavender Oil for Insect Bites

A drop of lavender oil will soothe a stinging or itching bite. Try lavender oil on itching leech bites.

LAVENDER AND HEADACHES

Sniff a few drops of lavender oil on a handkerchief. Mix a few drops of lavender oil with a few drops of olive oil and rub on aching temples; or take 2 drops on the tongue. Try a warm bath scented with lavender oil.

Headache Tea

Mix 1 part China green tea with 1 part camomile flowers, 1 part lavender flowers and ½ part yarrow flowers.
Make it in a teapot as you would ordinary tea. Pour on boiling water and leave it to brew for a couple of minutes.
  Headache tea can help relieve some types of migraine and is good for tension headaches. It is excellent at the end of a day of stress and worry. I keep headache tea in a jar ready to use whenever it is needed.

LAVENDER FOR THRUSH

A wash of warm lad's love tea mixed with lavender water was once used to cure vaginal thrush. Today, however, there are more effective remedies and as lad's love tea can be toxic if drunk, the recipe shouldn't be used for babies.

How to Dry Lavender

Lavender is the only herb that can be used fresh and for most purposes does not need to be dried. It can be placed in bunches in the cupboard or between sheets and not mark them. Lavender doesn't even have to be dried before it is added to potpourri.

To dry lavender for pretty posies, cut the spikes with scissors to keep them neat and hang the small bunches in an airy, dark place, such as a darkened room or a well-ventilated cupboard. If the room isn't absolutely dry, separate the stalks so they don't touch. Re-gather the posies when the flowers are so dry they crackle.

Lavender can also be dried in a conventional or a microwave oven. Place the lavender on brown paper to absorb the moisture and either microwave it on 'high' for 1 minute, or dry it in the oven at 50°C (120°F) for approximately 1 hour. This is a good way to dry lavender for use in cooking— it can then be crumbled off the stem and added to other ingredients.

Old-Fashioned Talcum Powder

MIX TOGETHER:

~ *2 parts cornflour, 2 parts rice flour, 1 part orris root, a few drops of lavender oil, and a few drops of vanilla.*

Keep in a sealed container, away from moisture. Dust on liberally.

WHERE TO KEEP DRIED LAVENDER

❧

in your clothes cupboards to deter moths and silverfish

❧

in your linen cupboard to sweetly scent the sheets and remove any mustiness

❧

place small posies in your shoes to freshen them

❧

in your handbag when it's not being used— the scent will waft out when you open the bag

❧

in food cupboards to repel food moths and weevils

❧

in the dog's bedding to help repel fleas

❧

keep a bowl of lavender potpourri above the toilet

LAVENDER COSMETICS

The distiled water of Lavender cleatheth the sight and putteth away all spottes, lentils, freckles and redness of the face if they be often washed therewith.

~

GERARD, *HERBAL*, 1597

Lavender Hair Conditioner

Sprinkle a few drops of lavender oil on your hair brush, and brush dry hair well. The oil won't make your hair greasy, but it will help condition it and keep it shiny and fragrant.

Lavender Bath Bag

Sprinkle 20 drops of lavender oil onto 3 cups rolled oats. Sew into a small sachet and use the bath bag instead of soap. It will both clean and perfume your skin and is good for pimples and grazes. It will last about a week if used every day.

Lavender Moisturiser

Simmer 1 cup of elder flowers and 1 cup of camomile flowers for 10 minutes. Cool. Add 20 drops of lavender oil and 1 tspn of almond oil. Keep in a small jar and smooth on the face at night.

This infusion can be thickened with a little beeswax, added while the mixture is hot.

Lavender Complexion Lotion
Simmer a large piece of comfrey root for 10 minutes. Add 1 cup of rose hips and simmer another 10 minutes. Strain. Add a large bunch of lavender flowers, put the lid on, and simmer for 3 minutes. Leave the lid on while the mixture cools, then decant and keep well stoppered. Dab on the lotion night and morning. This will help pimples, broken capillaries, prominent veins, insect bites and enlarged pores.

Lavender Bath Water
Simmer a large bunch of lavender in 2 cups of water, with the lid on the saucepan, for 5 minutes. Let the water cool before removing the lid or most of the fragrant oil will evaporate. Strain; add an equal amount of white wine vinegar to the liquid. Keep in a cool, dark place and use to perfume bath water.

GIFTS FROM LAVENDER

Lavender Honey

Fill a jar with chopped lavender flowers. Warm some honey so it flows
easily and pour it over the lavender. Leave for a few weeks, then heat
again and strain off the honey. This makes a fragrant and delicious
honey.

Wash Balls

Collect scraps of soap for a few months. Soak them in just enough water
to soften them. Add a few drops of lavender oil, a scattering of rolled
oats and a few well-chopped lavender flowers. Re-form the soap into
balls around the ends of long pieces of rope. Let them dry in the sun
and then package them attractively. They can be hung by the rope from
taps or shower fittings and are wonderfully scented and slightly
abrasive. (For a smoother soap ball, omit the oats and lavender flowers,
though an abrasive soap will make your skin glow and helps
circulation.)

Lavender Bubble Bath

For a gentle soak before bedtime, make a bubble bath by infusing 1 bottle of shampoo with 1 bunch of lavender flowers and a few drops of oil of lavender. Leave for 3 weeks, shaking every day. Strain the liquid, or simply place everything in a bottle, flowers and all.

Lavender Candles

Slowly melt 2 or 3 candles in a saucepan. Remove the wicks. Add a few drops of lavender oil to the melted wax as well as some chopped lavender flowers, if you wish. Dip each wick into the wax, hold it until the wax sets then repeat the process until the wick is again coated with the aromatic wax. If you prefer, you can sit the candle in a mould— if you can find one the right shape. Don't use too thick a mould, though, or the melted wax might flow inwards and cover the wick.
Lavender candles fill the room with fragrance.

Lavender Notepaper

Sprinkle notepaper with lavender oil— it won't mark the paper— then include dried lavender flowers when you rebox it. This makes a lovely gift.

Lavender Pillow

A lavender pillow is said to help you to sleep and to give you sweet dreams. It also helps prevent carsickness and nausea.

I make lavender pillows by stuffing fresh flowers into the loose stuffing of an existing pillow. The fragrance lasts for a couple of years. You can also scatter a few drops of lavender oil on your pillow each week.

A herb pillow is made by sewing the flowers into a cushion and adding other stuffing for extra softness. Other ingredients for a lavender pillow could include: dried hops, dried camomile flowers, dried peppermint leaves or lemon balm leaves (also good for nausea) or a little dried orange or lemon peel for extra fragrance. Orris root dusted into the herbs before they are sewn into the bag will add a gentle violet perfume, and help 'fix' the other perfumes.

Lavender Pot Holders

Lavender releases its perfume when it is warm so lavender pot holders and oven mitts are a lovely idea. Take a wide stretch of cotton wool and fold it over sprigs of lavender (they'll add extra insulation). Enclose the lavender and wadding in whatever material you choose for the holders— preferably a tough cotton or blanket material (never use synthetic fabric; it can burn or stick to hot dishes).

Lavender and Cumquat Gin

Place equal quantities of cumquats and lavender flowers in a bottle. Top up with 4 parts gin to 1 part sugar. Leave for 6 months. Eat the cumquats and drink the gin with soda water.

An Aphrodisiac Potpourri

~ 6 cups lavender flowers

~ 2 cups dried jasmine flowers

~ 3 cups dried pittosporum flowers

~ ½ cup sandalwood chips

~ 2 cups dried deep-red rose petals

~ ½ cup dried evergreen magnolia flowers

~ ½ cup dried violets

~ ½ cup orris root

Mix all the ingredients together. Keep in a sealed jar, and open on special occasions.

Lavender Fish

These are fun for children at bathtime. Take either a piece of foam or a piece of towelling and cut out 2 pieces in the shape of a fish. Sew most of the way around them, leaving an opening to insert the stuffing.

Fill the fish with lavender flowers (they can be either fresh or dried) and old scraps of soap, or even a new piece of soap. Sew up the opening. Children love to wash themselves with these scented fish.

Sweet Scented Bags to Lay with Linen

Eight ounces of damask rose leaves, eight ounces of coriander seeds, eight ounces of sweet orris root, eight ounces of calamus aromaticus, one ounce of mace, one ounce of cinnamon, half an ounce of cloves, four drachms of musl powder, two drachms of white loaf sugar, three ounces of lavender flowers, and some of Rhodium wood. Beat them well together and make them in small silk bags.

Mrs Hannah Glasse, *The Art of Cookery*, 1784

Lavender Aphrodisiacs

A Napoleonic Lavender Drink

Take equal parts of freshly brewed coffee, hot chocolate and musk
water, liberally sweetened with lavender sugar, and drink hot.
Napoleon is said to have drunk a glass of this before entering
Josephine's bedchamber.

Kissing Comfits

These originated in France, probably as breath fresheners.
Take fresh lavender spikes; cut off the stems. Dip the flowers first in
well-beaten egg white and then in icing (confectioner's) sugar (or
pounded ordinary sugar). While they are still damp, roll them on
nutmeg (which is a stimulant) and in powdered cherry stones. (These
can be crushed with a hammer, then a rolling pin.)
A more exotic fragrance can be attained by rolling them in powdered
ambergris.

Lavender and White Wine

Place one lavender spike, one slice of cucumber and several ice blocks in each glass.

Top with a chilled white wine – a chablis is excellent.

Lavender and Walnut Sauce

SERVES 2 AS A MAIN COURSE, OR IS A FIRST COURSE FOR 4

~ 5 cups (40 fl oz) of cream

~ 1 cup (8 fl oz) of chicken stock (stock cubes won't do)

~ 2 tbspns lavender flowers (these should be fresh, not dried and crumbly or they will be hard to remove from the sauce).

~half a cup of finely chopped walnuts

~ 1 tbspn chopped parsley

Simmer the cream and stock and lavender till it is reduced by half. Scoop out the lavender flowers. Add the walnuts and parsley; simmer again for five minutes. Serve over good quality pasta.

A LAVENDER POTPOURRI

LAVENDER VINEGAR

This can be used to rinse your hair (it will help repel — though not kill — head lice, and will also loosen their eggs). It is good dabbed on hot perspiring skin in summer.

Fill a jar with lavender, a few lemon verbena and mint leaves. Pour in hot vinegar, and seal the jar at once. Leave for three days. The vinegar may turn pale purple, but the colour will gradually fade and won't turn your hair or skin mauve. Strain; keep in a sealed jar in a cool dark place.

LAVENDER RUGS

These should be kept near the stove or fire. The oil will evaporate in the
heat and scent the room. Note: beware of sparks hitting the rug, as it is
flammable. Always use a fireguard with an open fire.

Stretch a length of hessian or other open material between two blocks
of wood, so the material is taught. Start at one end, and thread as many
spikes of lavender into the holes in the fabric as you can. Try to keep
the stalks on the other side pointing in the same direction.

When the mat is full of lavender, take a needle and thread and sew the
stalks onto the fabric. By now the 'blossom' side of the mat will be so
thick with lavender flowers that you won't be able to see the stitches
that hold up the stalks.

You may find your cat likes to sit on the lavender mat. Let it — it will
help get fid of fleas — and you will have a wonderfully scented feline
wandering through the house.

LAVENDER WOOD POLISH

Heat:
~ *2 cups beeswax*
~ *2 cups (16 fl oz) of turpentine*
~ *2 cups (16 fl oz) linseed oil or olive oil (olive oil is best for light coloured woods; linseed gives a richer, darker glow)*
~ *4 large bunches of lavender flowers, tied in a bunch*
Scoop out the flowers while the mixture is liquid. Place in a jar before it cools and sets.

A LAVENDER 'HAYBOX' OR 'NATURAL CROCKPOT'

Hayboxes are a means of slow, gentle cooking — and of conserving energy. Hay, or even dry grass, can be used, but dried lavender not only stores heat well, it also gives off a wonderful scent when the box is opened.

Choose a largish thick box with a well fitting lid
— or even a large pottery container. Place a layer
of dried lavender (stalks and all) in the bottom.

Now place a small casserole of stew or soup
ingredients, already brought to boiling point in
the container, on top of the lavender.

Quickly pack more lavender around the casserole,
around the sides and on top, then put the lid on.
For even better insulation wrap the whole thing
in blankets.

Now go off and do a day's work — or sit in the
garden and watch the hoverflies darting round
the lavender flowers. About ten minutes before
dinner time unwrap your casserole and reheat it.
This should be all the extra cooking it needs,
after a day in the 'haybox'.

Note: if you are cooking meat that might be
infected with pathogens or parasites, make sure
the casserole boils for at least twenty minutes
before you eat it.

Lavender Yoghurt

*This tastes slightly sweet,
though no sugar is added.*

~ *4 cups (1 l) of milk*
~ *a bunch of lavender flowers,
firmly tied together*
~ *2 tbspns natural yoghurt*

*Note: the yoghurt must be
fresh — less than a week old
— or the new yoghurt
will be sloppy.*

*Heat the milk and
lavender to simmering point.
Remove the lavender. When
the milk is cool enough to
touch it without being scalded,
add the yoghurt, stir it in,
then wrap the container in a
couple of teatowels and leave it
in a warm place overnight. (If
your house is cold, wrap a hot
water bottle up with the
container of yoghurt.)*

LAVENDER BEADS

As these warm up against your skin they release their perfume. They'll also help keep mosquitoes away.

~ 1 tbspn dried lavender flowers
~ 1 tspn lavender oil
~ 1 tbspn ground orris root
~ 1 tbspn gum tragacanth

Grind all ingredients together with a mortar and pestle and form into small round balls with your fingers. If the moisture needs more moistening, add more lavender oil or rose water or orange flower water. Pierce each small ball with a needle and let it dry in a dark cupboard, then string the beads together. The beads should be a rich purple, but the colour will gradually fade. If you don't want to buy gum tragacanth, most powdered gum will do.

LAVENDER WATER

Fill a small jar with lavender flowers. Top up with brandy. Shake well and leave for 48 hours; shake again; then strain into small bottles. Dab the lavender water on your temples for a headache, to refresh you, or just to enjoy the perfume.

Let's go to that house, for the linen looks white and smells of lavender, and I long to be in a pair of sheets that smell so...

~

IZAK WALTON, THE ANGLER, 1653

A Sweet-Scented Bath

Take of Roses, Citron peel, Sweet flowers, Orange flowers, Jessamy,
Bays, Rosemary, Lavender, Mint, Pennyroyal, of each a sufficient
quantity, boil them together gently and make a Bath to which add Oyl
of Spike six drops, musk five grains, Ambergris three grains.

John Middleton, *Five Hundred Recipes*, 1734

LAVENDER SPICE

PLACE IN A JAR:

~ *half a cup lavender flowers*

~ *1 tspn dried cloves*

~ *15 dried bay leaves*

Fill the jar with vinegar. Shake well; leave for 48 hours; shake again and strain.

This is a lovely scent when you don't want a cloying perfume. You can also use the mixture in the final rinse of your woollens, before you store them in winter, to help keep away moths.

LAVENDER BROOM

Brooms are traditionally made out of 'broom', because broom twigs won't burn when they sweep out the oven or the hearth. The tough stalks of English lavender also make excellent brooms. Trim off the flowers; separate the stalks into about ten small bundles; tie up each bundle firmly and trim the ends.

You can now tie all the bundles together around a long stick, a thick old-fashioned broom, or tie them along a shorter stick, with a long handle fitted in the middle for a 'pushing' broom— the shape more commonly used today.

LAVENDER PEST REPELLENT

Combine 2 tbspns lavender oil with 4 cups (1 l) of warm water in a
pump spray. Use the spray liberally around your house — on carpets,
curtains, bedding— it will help repel fleas, flies, mosquitoes, carpet
beetles, clothes moths and even ants.
Use the spray on your ironing too. It will make a boring job more
pleasant — and the clothes will be scented too.

LAVENDER MASSAGE OIL

This is said to soothe rheumatic pain, to help stiff joints and arthritis. It
is also lovely for a relaxing massage before you go to sleep, or if you
have the aches from flu or other fevers. A long lavender massage if you
think you might be getting a cold — and a good deep sleep afterwards
— may help to ward it off.
Either add 1 part lavender oil to 6 parts of massage oil; or pour your
massage oil over lavender flowers, and let it steep.

LAVENDER COMPRESS

Use this to soothe sprains and bruises. It's good for lower back pain,
sore knees, and pre-menstrual pain.
Combine equal parts of chopped lavender flowers with bran in a soft
old pillow case. You need only put about 10 cup fulls in the case, then
wrap the rest of the material around it.
Warm the case in the oven or microwave; keep it pressed against the
ache till it cools; then heat it again.

The wholesome sage, and lavender still gray
Ranke smelling rue, and cummin good for eyes
The roses, reigning in the pride of May
Sharp hishop, good for greens woundes remedies.

✢

Edmund Spenser, The Fate of the Butterfly

The Poetry of Lavender

Here's flowers for you;
Hot lavender, mints, savory, marjoram;
The marigold, that goes to bed wi' the sun,
And with him rises weeping.

✢

Shakespeare, The Winter's Tale

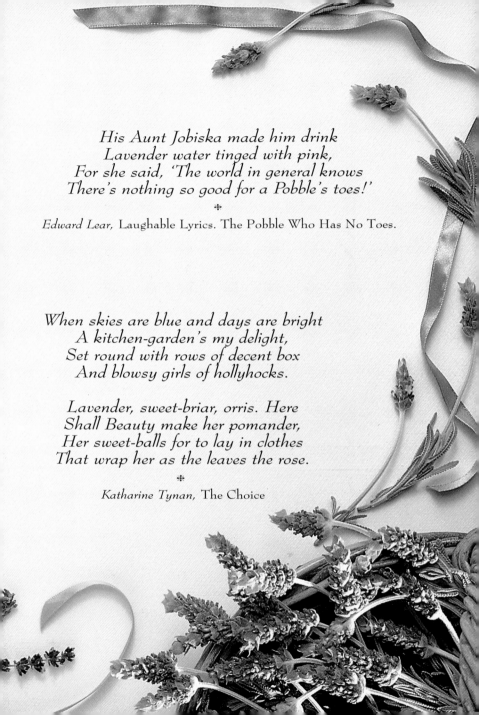

His Aunt Jobiska made him drink
Lavender water tinged with pink,
For she said, 'The world in general knows
There's nothing so good for a Pobble's toes!'

✳

Edward Lear, Laughable Lyrics. The Pobble Who Has No Toes.

When skies are blue and days are bright
A kitchen-garden's my delight,
Set round with rows of decent box
And blowsy girls of hollyhocks.

Lavender, sweet-briar, orris. Here
Shall Beauty make her pomander,
Her sweet-balls for to lay in clothes
That wrap her as the leaves the rose.

✳

Katharine Tynan, The Choice

ACKNOWLEDGMENTS

The publisher would like to thank the following organisations in NSW, Australia, for supplying various photographic props:

The Fragrant Garden, Erina

The Grosvenor Antique Centre, Lindfield

Home & Garden on the Mall, Sky Gardens, Sydney

Linen & Lace, Balmain

Wild Australia, Sky Gardens, Sydney

The Woollahra Antique Centre, Woollahra

~ ~ ~

PHOTOGRAPHY
Scott Cameron Photography Pty Ltd

FOOD STYLING
Lisa Hilton

COVER PHOTOGRAPHY
Ivy Hansen